"Social Media Millionaires: Proven Strategies for Success"

Introduction

Welcome to "Social Media Millionaires: Proven Strategies for Success". In today's digital age, social media has become an essential tool for businesses and individuals alike. It has opened up new opportunities to connect with audiences, build brands and grow wealth. The success stories of social media influencers and entrepreneurs have shown us just how powerful these platforms can be.

However, the road to becoming a social media millionaire is not always easy. There are many challenges to overcome and obstacles to navigate. In this eBook, we will provide you with proven strategies for success on social media. We will examine the tactics that have been used by some of the world's most successful social media millionaires, and explain how you can apply them to your own online journey. Whether you are an established business looking to increase your online presence, or an individual looking to build your personal brand and make a name for yourself, this eBook will provide you with the tools and information you need to succeed. So, let's get started on your journey to becoming a social media millionaire!

Index

1. Define your brand and target audience.

2. Create and consistently post high-quality content.
3. Utilize paid advertising to reach a wider audience.
4. Collaborate with other influencers and brands.
5. Utilize social media analytics to measure your success.
6. Stay up-to-date with the latest social media algorithms and trends.
7. Engage with your audience and respond to comments.
8. Utilize the power of video content, such as live streams and Instagram Stories.
9. Focus on building a strong personal brand.
10. Invest in professional photography and videography equipment
11. Utilize the power of social media influencer marketing.
12. Build a community around your brand and engage with them regularly.
13. Offer exclusive content to your followers.
14. Utilize social media platforms beyond just Instagram and Facebook.
15. Never stop learning and experimenting with new strategies.

Chapter 1
Define your brand and target audience.

Defining your brand and target audience is one of the most important steps in building a successful social media presence. Without a clear understanding of who you are and who your audience is, it will be difficult to create content that resonates and grows your following. Here is a comprehensive guide on how to define your brand and target audience for social media success.

Start with your brand: Your brand is more than just your logo or tagline. It's the essence of who you are, what you stand for, and what you offer to your audience. When defining your brand, consider your values, mission, and unique selling proposition. What sets you apart from others in your industry? What do you want to be known for? Answering these questions will help you create a clear and consistent brand message that will attract your ideal audience.

Know your target audience: Understanding your target audience is crucial for creating content that speaks to their needs and interests. Consider the demographics of your audience, such as their age, location, income, and education level. Also, think about their pain points, hobbies, and the types of content they enjoy consuming. Utilize social media analytics and tools such as surveys and polls to gather information about your audience.

Create a buyer persona: A buyer persona is a fictional representation of your ideal customer. It takes the information you have gathered about your target audience and puts a face and a name to it. This can help you create a more personal and targeted marketing strategy.

Utilize your brand and target audience in your content: Once you have defined your brand and target audience, it's time to put that information into action. Use your brand message and the interests of your target audience to create content that resonates with them. For example, if your target audience is interested in health and wellness, you might create content around healthy recipes, workout tips, and wellness products. Consistently incorporating your brand and target audience into your content will help you build a strong and loyal following.

In conclusion, defining your brand and target audience is an essential step in building a successful social media presence. By understanding who you are and who your audience is, you can create content that resonates and grows your following. Utilize the information you have gathered to create a clear brand message and a targeted marketing strategy. With a strong brand and a clear understanding of your target audience, you will be well on your way to social media success.

Chapter 2
Create and consistently post high-quality content

Creating and consistently posting high-quality content is essential for building a strong and engaged following on social media. The content you create will define your brand and help you connect with your target audience. Here is a comprehensive guide on how to create and consistently post high-quality content for social media success.

Start with a content strategy: A content strategy will help you stay organized and focused on your goals. Consider the types of content you want to create, the frequency of your posts, and the platforms you will use. You should also consider the audience you want to reach and the message you want to convey with your content.

Create a variety of content: Mixing up the types of content you create will keep your audience engaged and interested. Consider using a combination of text, images, videos, and live streams to create a well-rounded content plan. Experiment with different formats to see what works best for you and your audience.

Make sure your content is high-quality: The quality of your content is just as important as the quantity. Make sure your images and videos are clear and well-lit, and your text is well-written and free of errors. Utilize professional photography and videography equipment if necessary to enhance the quality of your content.

Post consistently: Consistency is key when it comes to posting content on social media. Choose a posting schedule that works for you and stick to it. This will help you build a strong following and establish a routine for your audience.

Utilize social media trends: Stay up-to-date with the latest social media trends and incorporate them into your content plan. For example, Instagram Reels have become increasingly popular, so consider using them to reach a wider audience.

Engage with your audience: Encourage engagement by asking questions, responding to comments, and creating interactive content. Engagement is key to building a strong and loyal following.

In conclusion, creating and consistently posting high-quality content is essential for building a successful social media presence. By developing a content strategy, using a variety of formats, and posting consistently, you can establish a strong brand and connect with your target audience. With a focus on quality and engagement, you will be well on your way to social media success.

Chapter 3
Utilize paid advertising to reach a wider audience.

Paid advertising is a powerful tool for businesses looking to reach a wider audience and promote their brand, products, or services. Paid advertising refers to the use of paid media channels, such as search engines, social media platforms, and online publications, to reach a target audience.

One of the main benefits of paid advertising is the ability to reach a large, targeted audience quickly and effectively. By utilizing paid advertising, businesses can reach their target audience at scale, without having to rely on organic growth methods such as search engine optimization or word-of-mouth marketing.

Another key benefit of paid advertising is the ability to measure and track the success of campaigns. This is possible because paid advertising platforms, such as Google AdWords and Facebook Ads, provide detailed analytics and reporting tools that allow businesses to track key metrics, such as impressions, clicks, conversions, and return on investment.

In order to effectively utilize paid advertising, businesses must first understand their target audience. This involves conducting market research and gathering data on the demographics, interests, and behavior patterns of their target audience. With this information, businesses can create highly targeted advertising campaigns that are more likely to reach and engage their target audience.

Once businesses have a clear understanding of their target audience, they can then select the right advertising platforms and channels to reach them. For example, businesses targeting a B2B audience might consider using LinkedIn Ads, while businesses targeting a consumer audience might consider using Facebook Ads. Additionally, businesses should consider the type of content they will use in their advertising campaigns, such as text, images, or video, and how they will structure their campaigns, such as using display ads, sponsored posts, or influencer marketing.

Another important consideration when utilizing paid advertising is budget. Businesses should set a clear advertising budget that aligns with their goals and objectives, and allocate resources accordingly. This will help ensure that advertising campaigns are effective and deliver the desired results.

In conclusion, utilizing paid advertising is an effective way for businesses to reach a wider audience and promote their brand, products, or services. By understanding their target audience, selecting the right advertising platforms and channels, and utilizing data and analytics to measure the success of campaigns, businesses can create highly targeted and effective advertising campaigns that drive results.

Chapter 4
Collaborate with other influencers and brands.

Collaborating with other influencers and brands can help you expand your reach and connect with a wider audience on social media. By working together, you can tap into each other's networks, share resources, and create unique content that benefits both parties. Here is a comprehensive guide on how to collaborate effectively for social media success.

Identify potential partners: Start by identifying influencers and brands that align with your values and mission. Look for those who have a similar target audience and a complementary brand message. Utilize tools such as social media analytics and influencer databases to help you find potential partners.

Reach out and build relationships: Building relationships with other influencers and brands is key to successful collaborations. Start by reaching out to those you are interested in working with and engage with their content. Show genuine interest in their brand and what they have to offer.

Consider your goals: Before entering into a collaboration, consider your goals and what you hope to achieve. Are you looking to expand your reach, increase brand awareness, or create unique content? Having clear goals in mind will help you choose the right partners and ensure a successful collaboration.

Create a win-win scenario: Collaborations should be a win-win scenario for both parties. Consider what each party can bring to the table and how you can work together to achieve your goals.

Communicate openly and effectively: Open and effective communication is crucial for successful collaborations. Establish clear lines of communication and regularly touch base with your partner to ensure the collaboration is on track.

Promote each other: When working with other influencers and brands, it's important to promote each other's content and platforms. Share each other's posts, tag each other in your stories, and include each other in your content. This will help expand your reach and increase brand awareness for both parties.

In conclusion, collaborating with other influencers and brands can be a powerful tool for expanding your reach and connecting with a wider audience on social media. By building relationships, communicating effectively, and promoting each other, you can create successful and impactful collaborations that benefit both parties. With a focus on creating win-win scenarios and achieving your goals, you will be well on your way to social media success.

Chapter 5
Utilize social media analytics to measure your success.

Social media analytics is the process of gathering, measuring, and analyzing data from social media platforms to evaluate the performance and impact of a company's social media presence. By utilizing social media analytics, companies can gain valuable insights into their target audience, track their social media performance, and measure the success of their campaigns.

One of the key benefits of using social media analytics is that it allows companies to better understand their target audience. By analyzing data such as the demographics, interests, and behaviors of their followers, companies can tailor their content and campaigns to better meet the needs and interests of their target audience. This can help increase engagement and drive more conversions.

Another benefit of social media analytics is that it allows companies to track the performance of their social media campaigns. For example, they can track the reach, engagement, and conversion rates of their posts and advertisements, and compare these metrics to their competitors. This information can be used to optimize future campaigns and ensure that resources are being allocated effectively.

One of the most important metrics to track in social media analytics is engagement. This includes metrics such as likes, comments, shares, and mentions. Engagement is a key indicator of the success of a company's social media presence, as it shows how well their content is resonating with their target audience.

Companies can use this information to identify the types of content that perform best and to make changes to their strategy as needed.

Another important metric to track is reach, which refers to the number of people who have seen a company's content. Reach is important because it gives companies an idea of how many people are being exposed to their brand. Companies can use reach data to determine the effectiveness of their content distribution strategies and to make changes as needed.

Social media analytics can also be used to track conversions, or the number of people who take a specific action after seeing a company's content, such as making a purchase or signing up for a newsletter. This information is valuable because it provides insight into the ROI of a company's social media efforts and can be used to optimize future campaigns.

In addition to these metrics, companies can use social media analytics to track the sentiment of their content. This involves analyzing the tone and emotions expressed in comments and mentions, and can provide valuable insights into how people feel about a company's brand. Companies can use this information to make changes to their content and campaigns as needed.

However, while social media analytics can provide valuable insights, companies must be careful to use the right metrics and to interpret the data correctly. For example, it is easy to become focused on metrics such as likes and followers, but these metrics do not necessarily reflect the success of a company's social media presence. It is important to look at a variety of metrics and to understand how they relate to a company's overall goals and objectives.

In conclusion, social media analytics is an essential tool for companies looking to measure the success of their social media presence. By analyzing data from social media platforms, companies can gain valuable insights into their target audience, track the performance of their campaigns, and make data-driven decisions to optimize their social media strategy. While social media analytics can provide valuable information, companies must be careful to use the right metrics and to interpret the data correctly to ensure that they are getting the most out of their social media efforts.

Chapter 6
Stay up-to-date with the latest social media algorithms and trends

Staying up-to-date with the latest social media algorithms and trends is crucial for success on these platforms. Social media algorithms are constantly changing, and new trends are emerging all the time. By staying informed, you can ensure that your content is being seen by your target audience and that you are using the latest tactics to grow your following. Here is a comprehensive guide on how to stay up-to-date with the latest social media algorithms and trends.

Follow industry leaders: Following influencers, experts, and industry leaders in the social media space will help you stay informed about the latest trends and algorithms. Read their blogs, listen to their podcasts, and follow them on social media to stay up-to-date with the latest news and insights.

Subscribe to social media updates: Many social media platforms provide updates and news on their algorithms and features. Make sure you are subscribed to these updates and read them regularly to stay informed.

Participate in social media communities: Joining social media communities and forums will give you access to a wealth of information and resources on the latest trends and algorithms. Engage in discussions, ask questions, and share your own insights to stay up-to-date with the latest developments.

Experiment with your content: One of the best ways to stay up-to-date with the latest algorithms and trends is to experiment with your content. Try new formats, features, and tactics, and see what works best for your audience. This will help you stay ahead of the curve and find new ways to reach your target audience.

Stay adaptable: Social media algorithms and trends are constantly evolving, so it's important to stay adaptable and flexible in your approach. Be open to trying new things and adjusting your strategy as needed to ensure success on these platforms.

In conclusion, staying up-to-date with the latest social media algorithms and trends is essential for success on these platforms. By following industry leaders, participating in social media communities, experimenting with your content, and staying adaptable, you can stay informed and ahead of the curve. With a focus on learning and adapting, you will be well on your way to social media success.

Chapter 7
Engage with your audience and respond to comments

Engaging with your audience and responding to comments is a crucial aspect of social media success. By connecting with your followers and responding to their comments, you can build a community of engaged and loyal fans. This will help you increase brand awareness, establish credibility, and grow your following on social media. Here is a comprehensive guide on how to effectively engage with your audience and respond to comments.

Be proactive: Make an effort to actively engage with your audience by starting conversations, asking questions, and responding to comments. The more you engage with your followers, the more likely they are to stay interested and engaged with your content.

Respond to comments in a timely manner: Responding to comments in a timely manner is crucial for effective engagement. Aim to respond to comments within a few hours or, at the latest, the next day. This will help you establish a reputation for being responsive and engaged with your audience.

Be friendly and approachable: When engaging with your audience, it's important to be friendly and approachable. Use a conversational tone, be personable, and show genuine interest in your followers and their comments.

Encourage interaction: Encourage interaction and engagement by asking open-ended questions, hosting quizzes and polls, and running contests and giveaways. This will help you build a community of engaged followers and keep your content relevant and interesting.

Handle negative comments with grace: Negative comments and criticism are a part of any social media presence. It's important to handle these comments with grace and professionalism. Respond in a calm and respectful manner, and use negative feedback as an opportunity to learn and improve.

In conclusion, engaging with your audience and responding to comments is a crucial aspect of social media success. By being proactive, responsive, friendly, and encouraging interaction, you can build a community of engaged and loyal followers. With a focus on connection and engagement, you will be well on your way to social media success.

Chapter 8
Utilize the power of video content, such as live streams and Instagram Stories

Video content has become a powerful tool for businesses looking to engage with their target audience on social media. With the rise of platforms like Instagram, YouTube, and Facebook, video has become the preferred format for many consumers, allowing companies to reach a wider audience and build stronger relationships with their customers.

One of the most popular forms of video content is live streams. Live streams offer businesses a unique opportunity to interact with their audience in real-time, answering questions and providing a behind-the-scenes look at their brand. Live streams can also be used to showcase products or services, host events, or provide exclusive content to followers. By creating a sense of immediacy and urgency, live streams can help increase engagement and build a loyal following.

Instagram Stories is another powerful tool for businesses looking to reach a wider audience.

Instagram Stories allows companies to share short, ephemeral videos and images with their followers. This format is particularly effective for capturing the attention of younger audiences and for promoting events, products, and services. Instagram Stories also allows companies to add interactive elements, such as polls and quizzes, to further engage with their followers.

When creating video content, it is important to keep in mind that quality is key. Poorly produced videos can detract from a brand's image, while high-quality videos can help build credibility and trust. Businesses should invest in good equipment and editing software, and take the time to plan their video content to ensure that it effectively communicates their message.

Another important consideration when creating video content is the tone and style of the videos. Companies should aim to create videos that are engaging, entertaining, and that match their brand personality. This can help build a stronger connection with their target audience and make their videos more memorable.

Finally, it is important to consider the target audience when creating video content. Companies should tailor their videos to meet the needs and interests of their target audience, and consider factors such as age, location, and interests when deciding what type of content to create. By understanding their target audience, companies can create video content that is more likely to resonate with their followers and drive engagement.

In conclusion, video content, such as live streams and Instagram Stories, can be a powerful tool for businesses looking to reach a wider audience on social media. By creating high-quality, engaging, and relevant video content, companies can build stronger relationships with their customers and drive more conversions. However, businesses must be mindful of the quality and style of their videos, and must take the time to understand their target audience to ensure that their videos are effective.

Chapter 9
Focus on building a strong personal brand

Focusing on building a strong personal brand is crucial for success on social media. Your personal brand represents who you are, what you stand for, and what sets you apart from others. By developing a strong personal brand, you can increase your visibility, establish credibility, and attract the right audience to your content. Here is a comprehensive guide on how to focus on building a strong personal brand.

Define your brand: Start by defining your brand and what sets you apart from others. Consider your unique skills, experiences, and personality, and use this information to create a clear brand statement.

Establish a consistent visual identity: A consistent visual identity is crucial for building a strong personal brand. Choose colors, fonts, and imagery that align with your brand, and use them consistently across all your social media platforms.

Create high-quality content: High-quality content is the cornerstone of any strong personal brand. Make sure your content is well-researched, engaging, and consistent with your brand. This will help you establish yourself as a thought leader in your niche.

Be authentic: Authenticity is key when building a strong personal brand. Be yourself, share your personal experiences and opinions, and stay true to your values. This will help you connect with your audience and build trust.

Network and collaborate: Networking and collaborating with other influencers and brands can help you build your personal brand and increase your visibility. Look for opportunities to guest post, participate in collaborations, and attend events in your niche.

Track your progress: Regularly track your progress and assess the impact of your personal brand building efforts. Use tools such as analytics, surveys, and focus groups to evaluate your brand and identify areas for improvement.

In conclusion, focusing on building a strong personal brand is crucial for success on social media. By defining your brand, creating high-quality content, being authentic, networking and collaborating, and tracking your progress, you can establish yourself as a thought leader in your niche and attract the right audience to your content. With a focus on building a strong personal brand, you will be well on your way to social media success.

Chapter 10
Invest in professional photography and videography equipment

Investing in professional photography and videography equipment is crucial for businesses looking to improve the quality of their visual content and communicate their brand effectively. High-quality images and videos help build credibility and trust with customers, and can also be used to attract and engage with a wider audience.

When choosing photography and videography equipment, it is important to consider the specific needs of the business. For example, a business that specializes in product photography may require a different set of equipment compared to a business that specializes in event photography. Businesses should also consider factors such as budget, level of experience, and the type of content they want to create when making their equipment choices.

One of the most important investments that businesses can make is in a high-quality camera. A good camera is essential for capturing sharp, detailed images and videos, and for achieving the desired visual style. Professional cameras often have advanced features, such as adjustable aperture and shutter speed, which can be used to create more dynamic and creative images.

In addition to a camera, businesses may also want to invest in lenses, lighting equipment, tripods, and other accessories that can enhance the quality of their visual content. For example, a business may want to invest in a wide-angle lens for capturing expansive landscapes or interiors, or in a macro lens for capturing close-up details. Lighting equipment, such as softbox lights or ring lights, can help improve the quality of portraits and product photography, while tripods can help ensure stability when taking long exposures or shooting video.

Investing in professional video equipment is equally important for businesses looking to create high-quality video content. This may include cameras specifically designed for video, microphones, stabilizing equipment, and editing software. A good video camera should have advanced features, such as the ability to adjust focus and exposure, and the ability to capture high-resolution audio.

In addition to equipment, businesses may also want to invest in the services of a professional photographer or videographer. This can be especially useful for businesses that do not have the expertise or experience to create high-quality visual content themselves. Professional photographers and videographers can help businesses achieve their desired visual style and ensure that their content is of the highest quality.

In conclusion, investing in professional photography and videography equipment is crucial for businesses looking to improve the quality of their visual content and communicate their brand effectively. High-quality images and videos can help build credibility and trust with customers, and can also be used to attract and engage with a wider audience. Businesses should carefully consider their needs and budget when choosing photography and videography equipment, and may also want to consider investing in the services of a professional photographer or videographer to help them achieve their desired visual style.

Chapter 11
Utilize the power of social media influencer marketing

Social media influencer marketing is a powerful tool for reaching a wider audience and increasing brand visibility. By partnering with influencers, companies and brands can tap into their existing followers and engage with a new audience in an authentic and engaging way. Here is a comprehensive guide on how to utilize the power of social media influencer marketing.

Define your target audience: The first step in influencer marketing is to define your target audience. Consider the demographics, interests, and behaviors of your target audience and use this information to identify influencers who align with your brand.

Research influencers: Research and identify influencers who align with your brand and target audience. Look for influencers who have a strong following, high engagement rates, and a consistent and authentic brand message.

Partner with the right influencer: Choose an influencer who aligns with your brand, has a genuine following, and is a good fit for your target audience. Consider their rates, reach, and the type of content they typically produce when making your decision.

Develop a clear agreement: Before partnering with an influencer, develop a clear agreement that outlines the goals and expectations of the partnership. This agreement should include the type of content to be produced, the reach and engagement goals, and any compensation for the influencer.

Measure your success: Regularly measure the success of your influencer marketing campaign. Use tools such as analytics, surveys, and focus groups to evaluate the impact of your influencer marketing efforts and identify areas for improvement.

In conclusion, utilizing the power of social media influencer marketing can be a highly effective way to reach a wider audience and increase brand visibility. By defining your target audience, researching influencers, partnering with the right influencer, developing a clear agreement, and measuring your success, you can maximize the impact of your influencer marketing efforts and achieve your desired goals.

Chapter 12
Build a community around your brand and engage with them regularly

Building a community around your brand is an effective way to engage with your target audience and build strong relationships with your customers. A community can be thought of as a group of individuals who share a common interest or passion, and who are brought together by a common goal or purpose.

For businesses, building a community around their brand can have a number of benefits. For example, a strong community can help increase brand loyalty, drive more referrals and word-of-mouth marketing, and provide valuable insights into the needs and desires of customers. Additionally, a community can help businesses foster a sense of belonging and connection with their customers, and provide a platform for two-way communication and feedback. One of the key steps in building a community around your brand is to engage with your audience regularly. This can involve a number of activities, such as hosting events, creating and sharing content, and responding to customer inquiries and feedback. Companies should aim to create a sense of intimacy and connection with their audience, and make their community feel like a supportive and inclusive space. Another important consideration when building a community is to foster a sense of belonging. This can be achieved by creating content that resonates with your target audience and by encouraging them to participate in activities and events. For example, a business specializing in outdoor gear might create a series of content pieces that showcase their products in action and share tips and stories from their customers. This type of content can help build a sense of community by connecting customers with the brand and with each other.

Social media platforms can also be used to build and engage with a community. For example, companies can create a dedicated Facebook Group or Instagram account for their community, where they can share content, host live Q&A sessions, and connect with customers on a more personal level. Additionally, companies can use social media to promote events and encourage customers to share their own stories and experiences with the brand.

In conclusion, building a community around your brand is a powerful way to engage with your target audience and build strong relationships with your customers. By fostering a sense of belonging and regularly engaging with your audience, businesses can create a supportive and inclusive space that can drive brand loyalty, referrals, and valuable customer insights. Companies should consider using a combination of events, content creation, and social media to build and engage with their community, and should always aim to make their customers feel valued and heard.

Chapter 13
Offer exclusive content to your followers

Offering exclusive content to your followers is a great way to increase engagement and foster a sense of community among your audience. By providing valuable and unique content, you can incentivize followers to stick around and engage with your brand on a deeper level. Here is a comprehensive guide on how to offer exclusive content to your followers.

Define your exclusive content: The first step in offering exclusive content is to define what type of content you want to offer. Consider the interests and preferences of your audience, and create content that aligns with their needs. This can include behind-the-scenes access, special promotions, early access to new products, and more.

Use social media platforms: Utilize social media platforms such as Instagram, Facebook, and Twitter to offer exclusive content to your followers. These platforms provide an easy and accessible way for you to connect with your audience and share exclusive content.

Provide value: The key to offering successful exclusive content is to provide value to your followers. Ensure that your exclusive content is high-quality, informative, and relevant to your audience.

Engage with your audience: Engage with your audience and respond to comments, questions, and feedback. This will help you build a deeper relationship with your followers and ensure that they feel valued and appreciated.

Track your success: Regularly track the success of your exclusive content and assess the impact of your efforts. Use tools such as analytics, surveys, and focus groups to evaluate your content and identify areas for improvement.

In conclusion, offering exclusive content to your followers is a great way to increase engagement and foster a sense of community among your audience. By defining your exclusive content, utilising social media platforms, providing value, engaging with your audience, and tracking your success, you can create a loyal and engaged following that will help drive your social media success.

Chapter 14
Utilize social media platforms beyond just Instagram and Facebook

Social media platforms extend beyond just Instagram and Facebook, and it's important to utilize these other platforms to reach a wider audience and increase brand visibility. Here is a comprehensive guide on how to utilize social media platforms beyond just Instagram and Facebook.

Identify your target audience: The first step in utilizing other social media platforms is to identify your target audience. Consider the demographics, interests, and behaviors of your target audience, and use this information to identify platforms that align with your brand.

Research platforms: Research and identify platforms that align with your brand and target audience. Look for platforms that have a strong following, high engagement rates, and a consistent and authentic brand message.

Choose the right platforms: Choose platforms that align with your brand, have a genuine following, and are a good fit for your target audience. Consider the type of content that is typically produced on each platform, as well as the audience demographics, when making your decision.

Develop a strategy: Before utilizing new platforms, develop a strategy that outlines your goals and expectations. This strategy should include the type of content to be produced, the reach and engagement goals, and a plan for regularly engaging with your audience on each platform.

Measure your success: Regularly measure the success of your efforts on each platform. Use tools such as analytics, surveys, and focus groups to evaluate the impact of your social media efforts and identify areas for improvement.

In conclusion, utilizing social media platforms beyond just Instagram and Facebook can be a highly effective way to reach a wider audience and increase brand visibility. By identifying your target audience, researching platforms, choosing the right platforms, developing a strategy, and measuring your success, you can maximize the impact of your social media efforts and achieve your desired goals. Examples of platforms beyond Instagram and Facebook include

TikTok, Twitter, LinkedIn, Pinterest, and Snapchat. Each platform offers unique features and a unique audience, so it's important to choose the right platforms for your brand and target audience.

Chapter 15
Never stop learning and experimenting with new strategies

In today's fast-paced business environment, it's essential to never stop learning and experimenting with new strategies in order to remain competitive and successful. In order to succeed in today's rapidly changing market, businesses must be open to new ideas and flexible in their approach.

One key aspect of continuous learning and experimentation is staying up to date on industry trends and best practices. This can involve attending conferences, workshops, and webinars, as well as reading trade publications and following thought leaders in the industry. By staying informed about the latest developments, businesses can identify new opportunities and develop strategies that are relevant and effective.

Another important aspect of continuous learning is experimenting with new strategies. This involves trying new approaches and testing new ideas to see what works and what doesn't. For example, a business might experiment with a new marketing campaign, a new pricing strategy, or a new product offering. By testing and experimenting with new strategies, businesses can identify what works best and make informed decisions about how to move forward.

In addition to continuous learning, it's also important for businesses to embrace change and be open to new ideas. This means being willing to challenge the status quo and consider new approaches, even if they are different from what has been done in the past. For example, a business might experiment with new technologies or embrace new business models, such as a subscription-based model, in order to better serve their customers.

One way to encourage continuous learning and experimentation is to create a culture of innovation within the company. This can be achieved by promoting a mindset of continuous improvement, encouraging employees to suggest new ideas and approaches, and investing in training and development opportunities. By creating a culture of innovation, businesses can foster a supportive environment where experimentation and learning are encouraged and valued.

In conclusion, never stopping learning and experimenting with new strategies is essential for businesses looking to remain competitive and successful in today's rapidly changing market. By staying up to date on industry trends and best practices, experimenting with new strategies, embracing change, and creating a culture of innovation, businesses can identify new opportunities, make informed decisions, and continuously improve their approach.

www.ingramcontent.com/pod-product-compliance
Lightning Source LLC
Chambersburg PA
CBHW040342220526
45473CB00009B/2767